Anton Yakovlev

CHRONOS DINES ALONE

SurVision Books

First published in 2018 by
SurVision Books
Dublin, Ireland
www.survisionmagazine.com

Copyright © Anton Yakovlev, 2018

Design © SurVision Books, 2018

ISBN: 978-1-912963-01-0

This book is in copyright. No part of this publication may be reproduced, stored in a retrieval system or transmitted in any form or by any means without the prior permission in writing from the publisher.

Acknowledgements

Across the Margin: "The Man Who Remixed Your Soul," "The Farewell"

Construction Magazine: "Swim Through It for a While"

E-Verse Radio: "One Day This Year"

First Literary Review East: "When Balloons Finally Departed"

Fjords Review: "Insomnia," "Bum Hamlet"

Gramma Poetry: "Transmissions," "One Must Imagine Her Happy"

The Hopkins Review: "California"

Local Knowledge: "Because You're Young"

Mud Season Review: "Happy Hour"

Pangyrus: "Effigyville"

Peacock Journal: "Today Is a Mistake in Any Cosmology"

The Rutherford Red Wheelbarrow: "On a Red Line Train to Braintree," "Letheside Public Library"

Resist Much / Obey Little: "In the Future"

SurVision: "Demon Daycare," "Homecoming"

UCity Review: "The Fear Machine"

CONTENTS

California   5
Effigyville   6
Because You're Young   9
On a Red Line Train to Braintree   10
Demon Daycare   12
Happy Hour   14
The Man Who Remixed Your Soul   17
The Fear Machine   18
Insomnia   20
Today Is a Mistake in Any Cosmology   23
Transmissions   24
The Farewell   26
When Balloons Finally Departed   28
One Must Imagine Her Happy   29
Swim Through It for a While   30
Homecoming   32
Letheside Public Library   34
In the Future   36
One Day This Year   38
Bum Hamlet   40

California

Someone's been shot. Someone's still trying to break
the invisible wall. We all live in the yellow.
You take the bus without pain. *A perfect Victorian*
conclusion to a terrifying Sunday night. I have postcards
of you smiling. What a shock to find you in love—
the gratitude of it, the warmed-up park benches,
the Zen of coming back to the same ice cream.
Our hearts won't leave us alone. Well, we weren't trying
to be alone. We're too focused on immortality,
which means reflection in the eyes of the not-yet-dead.
We stare at lava. Sometimes we throw money at grief.
If we had questions, they've all been drowned.
You were good at shutting the shutters.
Today California almost reached them with a paintbrush.
Old movies love us without bringing back our friends,
now dead, who watched them with us. Of course,
we are also deader now, even in love. The TV show about
the vodka-drinking policeman playing basketball with a fish
now feels like a quirky mentor, and we start crying.
When you hail the cab to the next moment,
don't forget to pick up your previous mind from the puddle,
just for archival purposes. I will never forget you.

Effigyville

When the old designer store downtown
went out of business and was razed to the ground,
the moldy crater where it had stood was adorned with posters
illustrating a luminescent housing development
that was about to be erected in its location,
so tall one could almost see England from its top floors.
But when the builders of the new structure went bankrupt,
the posters faded from the seasonal weather changes
and soon were no more than gaping metal boards.
To make some use of them, and to slightly alleviate
the heavy moods of old jewelers strolling the city streets
and ladies with aging dogs peeking out of handbags,
City Hall took charge and put up ornate watercolors
of the imploded designer store, back in its golden years.

Soon families with strollers readjusted their daily walks
to no longer avoid the downtown. The elegant toddlers
found themselves in a reverie, musing about the building
that used to stand there—an activity healthy enough
that no one objected when a similar set of posters
went up down the street, at the site of a former bookstore
that had suddenly run out of customers.

A waterfront natural history museum was next to go.
Its implosion was met with unforeseen geographic
cataclysms, a landslide making the waterfront

disappear along with the building. Nevertheless,
murals were erected, showing in splendid brushstrokes
the glory days of the museum and of the creatures there.

The oldest tavern in town closed down shortly thereafter.
Award-winning musicians were invited to play at its
    demolition,
timing their melodies with the metronome of the battering
    ram.
Soon there were resplendent pencil sketches around
demonstrating the tavern's unique Victorian architecture
and the fraternal spirit that had made its customers feel
    immortal.

The circus was next, then the zoo, then the opera house.
Law firms followed suit. Like a house of cards,
the casino folded. Jails were swiftly dismantled,
sometimes at night, to slow the onset of anarchy.
A house of worship was turned into a swimming pool,
but then there was no more water for people to swim in,
and all that was left was a brand new radiant mural
portraying the house of worship, while a small poster
of the swimming pool curled up near one of its corners.

City Hall was the last to fall: its grand edifice
was the hardest to sketch, so intricately it wove
various dead end corridors, visible even from
the outside of the building—a conscious metaphor
for the way they did business back when there was a city.

Finally, a great artist answered the call,
succeeded at painting the building—and then it was gone.

A cloud of old dust hovering over deserted streets,
the city of murals and posters stood silent in summertime,
offering no spin, no bias, no right way to think
to the amateur photographer that happened to wander
onto the old city streets one day, his battery fully charged.
He tried to take pictures but only took pictures of pictures,
and pictures of pictures had always interested him less
than any other pictures. So he jumped back in his car,
kicking up a cloud of sand with his all-wheel drive,
and turned his attention to the forest of reeds and ferns,
which reached much higher now than the highest penthouse.

Because You're Young

You try to paint your fence but get interrupted
by northern lights. You still remember the face
they resemble. Your latest attempt at fear
makes the boulders smile in spite of themselves.
You sit on them and dodge the out-of-control
diplodocus, still hoping to write a treatise
on his adorability. Ocean waves are woven
into affordable shawls. When you count sheep at night,
you still bother to name them. It's still a decade before
the first time you'll refer to your hometown
as a quartered corpse laid out over a meadow.
Genghis Khan isn't so bad. None of your past amputations
have set you back more than three hours. You think of
every black skyscraper as challenging the sky's philosophy
without working out the exact terms of
the challenge. The smell of old rags and the smell of
good errors give you the same pleasant nostalgia.
You just dig your toes deeper and talk to earthworms.
Your dog still tries to sharpen his teeth on cats.
A pizza is just a pizza. The sight of four horses
is not synonymous with rigor mortis.
You're still on a first-name basis
with saccharine. You can still turn into a bird
and smash without regret into your own glass.
Your driveway can become a painting at any moment
then turn into a spaceship built entirely of fire.
Your siblings' march into hell is always reversible.

On a Red Line Train to Braintree

The first time I saw the Grim Reaper,
he was right next to my foot. I mistook him for an oversize
    moth.
I was about to squash him but became curious.
He flew up, settled behind the woman
sitting directly in front of me on the train,
and started to inch his scythe toward her neck.
The woman shifted her shoulders.
The Grim Reaper looked quiet and even-keeled.
The passengers next to us saw him too,
but no one did anything and just smiled about it.
There was a poster hanging above the Reaper
with hefty postcards attached, to enroll at a community
    college.
A plan was born in my mind: pick a card and throw it at him.
That would cause a disturbance great enough
    that the Reaper would have to scram.
But an emotional song was playing on my iPod.
It was too much of a special moment.
Besides, in order to pick up that card
I would have had to lean in too close to the woman,
whose low-cut shirt was not all that well adjusted.
The Reaper never stirred, just inched his scythe closer.
The train came out of the tunnel, and the woman
started dialing her boyfriend on her iPhone
to tell him about the Grim Reaper that hovered behind her.

I was curious whether this would make the boyfriend
break up with her, or, on the contrary, offer
love and new jewelry; but it was too noisy to eavesdrop.
I hoped the woman would exit at the same station as I,
to see if the Reaper would follow her. But she didn't.
I had to go. She remained sitting, blade at her neck.
As I walked out, everyone on the train was commenting on
    the Grim Reaper,
husbands making sophisticated jokes to their wives and
    children,
translating some of the more difficult stuff for foreigners.
I came home and quickly fell asleep.
I did not dream of anything I had seen.
The next morning, looking through the *Metro* and *Phoenix*,
I looked for news of a subway death—but the papers
must have been sent to press too early to run the story.

Demon Daycare

For Bridget

Mildly mangled, they scoop
condemned milk from their pancake plates
and polka with dearly departed rattles
before sweating out an afternoon nap.

The substitute nanny
spits sulfur, disciplines
them with a ripped-out
Shakespeare signature.

Their formerly reddish eyes
bounce all over the playroom,
each pupil a moth.
From one pupil

a ballerina emerges
to embark on a romance whose vectors
point ever outward,
until the daycare center closes its doors.

They march home then, stoic mugs reflecting
in a Christian Science reflecting pool.
The ballerina grows weary.
The world can't stop saying no.

She scatters breadcrumbs,
but the rooftop birds
are gargoyles.
She rebuttons her vest.

She petitions the weather for a chariot,
but touchy Persephone has made a sign of the horns,
and every storefront mannequin
shuts her eyes.

Happy Hour

Your best friend is drinking himself to death
and you ask me if I know any hit men
you can hire for a mercy killing.

We're sitting in a steakhouse
enjoying two-for-one New York strips.

Before I get the chance to talk about hit men
you start to talk about Wagner.
You talk for twenty minutes about Wagner
but get all the details wrong.

I've never met your best friend.

  *

Your business suit looks like a paper airplane,
your scarf an army of moths.

Earlier, when I met you at the train,
you walked straight past me.

I've never met your best friend.

And you got all the details wrong.

So what can I do?

I talk to you about Wagner.
I correct your details.

I talk about the quintet
in *Die Meistersinger von Nürnberg*,
the way it soared right through the entire twentieth century
and settled on the windowsill of a small one-bedroom
    apartment
of an undertaker in East Berlin.

*

One year later, I run into you
and we reminisce about last year.

Turns out I heard almost nothing you said.

You told me about your best friend's criminal record.
You told me about his dead family.
You told me about the time he almost killed you with sleeping
    pills.

He's fine now.
He has a job and a moustache.
His house is listed in the Register of Historic Places.
He's getting married in October.

You've never forgiven me.

*

Too many people talk about "The Ride of the Valkyries"
like it's nothing.
Young parents with baby strollers walk through a dying
    downtown
and hum the fucking thing.

A coquette on social media
told me the other day
her life was as predictable as the overture to *Das Rheingold*.

Two Wagnerian cars collide on a circle.

I never saw the timetable
for the departure of your paper airplane.

The hills in the morning mist
look like your shoulders.

The Man Who Remixed Your Soul

I walked with you through Washington Square Park
transmitting the voice of God but you didn't notice

I set fire to the orange in your Manhattan
but all you wanted was to change the station

I called myself your life's signature oasis
but you drowned me in static

So then I buried myself in a potter's field
and you wouldn't stop spinning requiems

My ears had loved you even in your past life
but you jumped to the next track and got lost

By the time you came back the man who remixed
your soul had gotten permanently stoned

These days I try to spot you in every park
but the voice of God is all I hear

The Fear Machine

The fear machine stood in the corner of the theater
as we rehearsed our play.

It was covered in footsteps of different sizes.

It emitted the soft hum of an engine
still running after an accident.

Our two-person play had been written for us.

But the fear machine hummed in the corner
and "mango" came out like "mangled."

"Why are you sad?" came out like
"Why are you causing these circles under my eyes?"

After a while we were each other's serial killers.

"Admit it," I said. "It's *mango*."
"*You* choke on it!" you mouthed.

Stage right, the fear machine hummed:
"Give me a hug. Give me a hug. Give me a hug. Give me a
    hug. Give me a hug."

One day, the world didn't end.
The next day, we had no philosophy.

A week later, our play was no good.
Two weeks later, it was streamed in high definition.

Fear machines bounced about the cinemas,
hitting the viewers.

           We tried to laugh,
but our schadenfreude wasn't convincing.

Thirty years later, we still keep our halves of
the fear machine, wishing they'd held together.

Insomnia

Pictures of ruffled hair.
      Pictures of skyward eyes.

    I am too much with you.
        Pupils drift sideways.

We drift to flashes of orange, a floodlit alley.
      Constellations play
    restless checkers outside.

    I am too much with you. You find me
in your roaster chicken. You see me
      in a splashy helicopter. Pictures

        of hair growing out
      of pupils. You're a prophet

    who goes to the bathroom to freshen up,
      apply lip gloss, apply shadow.
When you reemerge, no one recognizes you.

    They declare you missing,
    call a search party.

    You join it too, spend five hours
    looking for a missing prophet
    before realizing it's you.

I wasn't there to tell them who you were.
I wasn't there to tell yourself who you were. And yet

   I am too much with you.
I am in your every text message
    to all the blessed fuckers
       in the celestial bathtub.

         Pictures of curtsy.
Pictures of various escapes.

You want to find out more
     about your banshee parents
    by seeing them through my eyes.

I want to close my eyes, but my eyes are spotlights.

    Every spotlight is a thorn.

        Pictures of thorns.

  After you're found,
everyone in the search party acts like
      you don't exist.

  You just want to go off someplace
where people won't roll their eyes.

I don't roll anything, yet
    I am too much with you.

      A Möbius strip.

A cat left behind by the herd, you crash through the trees
        just as I set them on fire.

        You memorize silence.

Pictures of helicopters
      taken from behind eyelids.

    I am too much your prophet.
You scratch the air with my voice.

You speak to me through wooden fruit.

I align myself with a broken tree on the ground.

Insomnia runs in the blood of our greatest rivers.

      There is no stronger coffee
than the science fiction we've become.

Today Is a Mistake in Any Cosmology

Remember the ravens had a name for each of us?
Then we got on the bus and you told me
you didn't want to see me anymore.
I thought I had known the color of your hair.
We continued to call each other.
I was trying not to let my foot off the memory
of walking with you along the ocean,
dusk, and everyone buying fireflies at the market,
the band trying to finish their set
while the concert hall was being demolished.
I never loved the wrinkles around your eyes more.
I sent you flowers. Forgive me, I sent you flowers.
I bought plant food. Forgive me, it fell and spilled.

Transmissions

There was a time they said these things cheek-to-cheek.
Now, talking to her, his voice takes the shape of waves
and makes its way to the cell phone tower in Manchester-by-
    the-Sea,
built to look like an oversize mast in the middle of a marina.

From there it goes on to a redwood in Pennsylvania,
the only redwood that exists in the state.
Why they could not have shaped their cell phone tower
like a blue spruce, even Pan doesn't have a clue.

Onward, with barely noticeable static,
the silent waves of his words reach the Cross of Calvary
-shaped cell phone tower in the Bible Belt
then move to a citadel at a maximum security prison.

"I love you," he casually drops, and his sentiment reaches her
courtesy of a giant metal giraffe on a hill in front of a diner,
a war memorial with a double life, a whimsical out-of-
    commission lighthouse
that only men with mustaches are allowed to enter.

"I almost ran over a toddler today. I cried," she confesses
via gigantic deer antlers in a nature preserve,
a purple hundred foot cactus in an oasis,
the lone horn of a jumbo rhinoceros at the top of a
    rollercoaster.

Tirelessly she relates how her family members enslave her,
or so she thinks, her voice transmitted by turrets
on haunted Victorian mansions, giant chips on top of casinos
and a tall copper flame-shaped sculpture in the middle of a
    columbarium.

"I wish you were here. I just made some more instant coffee,"
a flagpole with an upside down American flag transmits
on a day of a quickly-developing national crisis.
"I still don't like cats," she insists, through several obelisks.

They have been talking for over an hour now, and he is tired.
"Goodbye," he says abruptly. She asks him about his day.
"Goodbye," he repeats. She keeps talking. She is unstoppable.
"Goodbye," he says again—but stays on the line.

The Farewell

The vistas are visible for miles.

Your curls form letters,
happenstance labyrinths of cursive.

Mahler's *Songs of the Earth* play on the radio.

Soon, ocean waves will turn saber.
Skulls will fill with their foam.

A couple of tables away, Chronos dines alone.

Outside the café, horses on leave from Minotaur's posse
understand love much better than you might think.

  *

We speak of the elegant way
doves hold lanterns in some historic downtowns,
your local Hercules who dips locusts in his mojitos,
the umbrellas of bareback coquettes,
the inexplicable sadness of noon,
the prestige of waterfalls,
the surging of ambrosial musical instruments,
my collection of dead lake snapshots,
your harbor's oversea shipments,

the garbage in our dictionaries,
our old days, our funny antiques,
our funny religions, our funny grizzly bears,
our century-long vigils, our too-cute minivan,
the telescope we used as a shovel,
the places we won't visit together,
the nothing of the sea and the everything of the nothing,
the salamanders who squeal, the chickens who see in azure,
the laid-off orchestra members who find bizarre flutes to
    master,
the people we'll have to meet,
the gods who misplace their business,
the headless impersonations of Albrecht Dürer.

Ocean waves are full of headless impersonations.

*

On his way back from the bathroom,
Chronos stops at our table and yaks
about his plan to build an escalator
in the middle of a nearby vineyard.

You blink once.

When Balloons Finally Departed

she ignored the sunset and gathered his letters, finding
she had lost most of them, and with them his thin hair,
his hands. Now everyone she had missed was returning
as antisocial birds. The clock misbehaved, rotten pulp
made music in the wind. She recoiled from rain, as if
the sky spat on her. Earths recombined themselves
in startling patterns. A lighthouse wandered around.
A panda walked into a bar and betrayed his country.
She couldn't tell the little boy from the river —
both had lucifers crawling out of their mouths.
She knew she couldn't stay off camera much longer.
She had to invent a new language they all would love
but no one would understand.

One Must Imagine Her Happy

Again he snowdrops out of her permafrost
and she replays last year's World Cup games
just to glimpse the tigers in the audience
they glimpsed together when they *were* together.

The tigers are binging on frozen yogurt—
she can see that quite clearly now.
Their smiles look like her own.
Death is parked off-campus.

Swim Through It for a While

The gallows stood at the lowest point of the valley, with no noose and no hangman. It showed up in every tourist's nighttime diary entry. Most people wondered about the person due to be executed, wondered about his or her whereabouts, and wished someone would remove the gallows before death could be carried out. No one wondered about the crime. A few hopped like rabbits to the bottom of the valley and drank coffee in the gallows' hollow shadow.

You were the only one who identified not with the condemned but with the gallows. Their loneliness and toughness fascinated you. Within a few seconds you started talking to me in the voice of the gallows, and waxed poetic about your resilience, standing there like that, listening to meteorites, always tempted to fall with them, always resisting the temptation.

Your eyes shone with an electric glow similar to the light bulbs in Isaac Asimov's basement. You wore a black jacket with a red diagonal line reminiscent of a slashed throat. Still speaking as the gallows, you attempted a prayer but messed up the Lord's name and unleashed a string of profanities so uncomfortable you almost tripped over a piece of rotten tree bark. "Good thing the gallows don't swear," I joked and ran my fingers through your hair, releasing long-forgotten rose petals. You hummed your favorite homage to Pallas.

Then you took out your flask and sipped cognac, consciously avoiding eye contact. A scholarly tourist approached us and started to hop around like a rabbit. I asked him if he was the condemned. He took off all his clothes and hopped toward the gallows, then right past them and the fuck away.

I don't remember everything that happened that day, couldn't tell you how much my pulse was, whether my blood pressure was at an acceptable level or whether I craved coffee like some black bear with a headache. I do remember your attempts to take on the shape of the gallows and cast a similar-looking shadow.

Much later you told me you had come with me to the valley on the recommendation of someone you secretly loved, a casual fan of outmoded execution devices with whom you had shared one coffee in the corner of a third-hand bookstore. You carried his third-hand book in your pocket. You had lost touch with him. It was in honor of your feelings for him that you wanted to become the gallows, to stand unshakable in the middle of a grassy plain.

I think back to the poses you struck, silhouetted against the bright lights of distant all-terrain vehicles. I'm no longer in touch with anyone who remembers you. The valley has been paved over. The gallows has been replaced with a museum of contemporary art. I drive to its parking lot, strip down to my bathing suit, plunge into the viscous macadam, and swim through it for a while.

Homecoming

You enter somber into the old mountain,
enter with donkeys, with doting neighbors, with
    chiropractors.
You march through the bars, a caricature
of wisdom, a ringing bell.

You craft a dirge, call down the pale rain,
wash yourself in watery echo,
take center stage and collapse.
Each night you become your own audience.

You're confident you'll always find ways to thrive,
though only as much as a crow in a coliseum.
Austerity acorns collect under the sad trees
until you drink yourself into optimism.

The East River Ferry is rechristened as *De Profundis*.
Brittle-boned pigs play football over your lifetime.
In truth, this is all a store front
with plastic fruit microwaved to look more alive.

It's joust day, folks. You joust against your own faces.
The fans place bets, but mostly bet on the waterfall
that chimes behind you. Meanwhile, from up above,
some deity sees the whole scene as a kind of gourmet
    casserole.

You miss the people you miss, then hop on their trolley.
Do you remember your first attempts at a tango?
You pepper spray your best friend to bluntly welcome your
    autumn,
then watch forgiveness unfold its indirect wings.

Your eyes tell the story.

Letheside Public Library

From high up in the clouds, only a few books can sing:
mainly those whose eyes have remained unchewed,
whose aim is to draw out catharses from our own internal
    libraries
until we no longer have a single numb nerve.

On the whole, this fashion suits me. I become a high-roller.
Wine flows from God's aorta,
and blessed manuscripts descend
from the arboreta of my subjective perception.

Yet I have no north. My narratives flail.
Only light separates the garden from the escape.
I'm a prettified second-hander rubbing the graves
of rumbling luminaries.

There are so many exotic tragedies in those books,
so many single dinosaurs desperate to double-date,
so many dead, out smoking in timeless gowns—
you lose sight of all the disgruntled modernists just wishing
    for simple sex.

I hope things slow down before long.
I hope I'll get a supporting part in the play of cloth-bound
    cotton pages—
hell, even glimpse my own books in some reader's wardrobe.
But for now I can only take baths in the columbarium.

How many will shine blue-chip?
How many of us will run off the edge of the cliff
and emerge as useful containers
for a handful of adjustable tears?

Does every out-of-body experience require
a martini of horror? Pour me some tea instead.
Pass me that park bench. We split and split every pillar,
but still they stand. There is even some tenderness that
    survives.

Don't bum me out, old master. I'll shine a light on you yet.
The world will warp enough to show itself as millennia—
or at least as a vineyard lake, where the silk fish have swum
too many circles to concern themselves with extinction.

In the Future

In the future every car will come with a tree
affixed to its exhaust pipe,
soaking up the carbon dioxide.

Emissions inspections will be conducted by gardeners
verifying the health of the tree.

Boys taking girls to the prom
better take care of their tree,
lest they face the girls' fathers
watching their exhausts from second floor windows.

Fire brigades will compete in friendly olympics
where juries measure the size of the giant trees
on the back of their trucks
and firemen run high-risk demonstrations
of how they can put out fires without burning their tree.

The trees will be grown in high-security gardens,
artificially engineered to speed up their photosynthesis,
absorbing thousands of times more carbon dioxide
than the trees you see today on Park Ave.

It will be considered good luck
to have garden gnomes in your car.
The Bergen County Garden Gnome Manufacturers

will suddenly become a giant of industry.
Garden gnome heirs will put on airs
and open art galleries.

In the future every town will have windmills
lining the streets where trees used to be.
Streets will be painted white:
white asphalt absorbs less heat.
Strong sunglasses will be a must for motorists.

And in the sky, an artificial Zeus
will be adding clouds in strategic places
to dim the world just enough that glaciers come back
and polar bears can drink their sodas in peace.

You won't live till that day, and neither will I.
Our great-great-grandchildren
will be researching their ancestry
and visiting the sites of our townhouses,
nostalgic for the carelessness and the recklessness,
the wilderness and the randomness,
the horse farms and the unanticipated sequoias
that sprouted wherever they pleased,
unattached to the back of a car.

They will say, "I wish I could speak with them"
and post old digital photos in their live journals,
while trained ravens glide by outside
with solar batteries on their wings.

One Day This Year

The tower of quarters intact on a loved one's stair
No one to cut your heart out in the basement
Anonymous suburbia somehow feeling
An unbroken parade of noiseless fire trucks
A warm burger during a bomb scare
Gift cards gifted on time
People forgiving strangers over the phone
The frameable small waves on the Neva river
Listening to Tchaikovsky on Tchaikovsky Street
A TV stakeout in the company of both parents
An amendment to a Rorschach monster
An obscure intelligence finding a home
A warm nearby forest never explored until today
A crutch given away
The car starting
A car pulling out of the driveway
narrowly avoiding the priceless flowers
The universal leash for every dog out there
The Pale Horse waving its hoof at the happy roller skater
without a plan to trample her
The lack of boulders on the beautiful lawn
The boulders arranged in personally meaningful patterns
Yellow flowers coming out
A life-affirming lecture by Winnie the Pooh
The one who matters the most recognizing your head is not
    filled with woodchips

The one who matters the most not watching the clock
A favorite soccer team doing pretty well
The incognito sports star on a chair lift
One day this year we don't hear of stars burning out
The dog rescuing his master from the Grand Canyon
The ATVs gliding noiselessly through a picturesque forest
The departure of the Id Iago
The business card of a standoffish pioneer

Bum Hamlet

Moving forward, none of our stories will fill
or empty any bottles. Newsprint will continue to yellow.
The captain under your window will continue to throw
tentative tritons your way,
never reaching your ears through glass.
A Grim Reaper impersonator will major in rocking boats
but, failing to secure an internship, move to Finland.

Only a black bear makes your home his home,
gliding over its non-trivial rooftop wires
with the ease of a cadaver giving up carbon isotopes.
Your fluency is rock-paper-scissors,
and your sleep is a braided Acheron.
Come out fighting, make a macadamia of yourself,
feed old bones into the steam locomotive.

I'm all eyes now. Your illusive harvests, your body décor,
the piñata zeitgeist of your collapsed balcony
have learned to sing harmony. Now where is your traffic jam?
Moving backwards through years of firework standoffs,
I've glimpsed your collapsing politics in that mirror,
don't you forget that. I've sliced through the spider webs.
We've walked across that field for a little while.

More poetry published by SurVision Books

Noelle Kocot. *Humanity*
 (New Poetics: USA)
 ISBN 978-1-9995903-0-7

Ciaran O'Driscoll. *The Speaking Trees*
 (New Poetics: Ireland)
 ISBN 978-1-9995903-1-4

Elin O'Hara Slavick. *Cameramouth*
 (New Poetics: USA)
 ISBN 978-1-9995903-4-5

Anatoly Kudryavitsky. *Stowaway*
 (New Poetics: Ireland)
 ISBN 978-1-9995903-2-1

George Kalamaras. *That Moment of Wept*
 ISBN 978-1-9995903-7-6

Christopher Prewitt. *Paradise Hammer*
 (Winner of James Tate Poetry Prize 2018)
 ISBN 978-1-9995903-9-0

Bob Lucky. *Conversation Starters in the Language No One Speaks*
 (Winner of James Tate Poetry Prize 2018)
 ISBN 978-1-912963-00-3

Sergey Biryukov. *Transformations*
Translated from Russian
(New Poetics: Russia)
ISBN 978-1-9995903-5-2

Maria Grazia Calandrone. *Fossils*
Translated from Italian
(New Poetics: Italy)
ISBN 978-1-9995903-6-9

Anton G. Leitner. *Selected Poems 1981–2015*
Translated from German
ISBN 978-1-9995903-8-3

Our books are available to order via
http://survisionmagazine.com/books.htm